Little Books of Guidance
Finding answers to life's big questions!

Also in the series:
What Do We Mean by 'God'? by Keith Ward
What Does It Mean to Be Holy Whole? by Timothy F. Sedgwick
Why Suffering? by Ian S. Markham
How to Be a Disciple and Digital by Karekin M. Yarian
What Is Christianity? by Rowan Williams
Who Was Jesus? by James D. G. Dunn
Why Go to Church? by C. K. Robertson
How Can Anyone Read the Bible? by L. William Countryman
What Happens When We Die? by Thomas G. Long
What About Sex? by Tobias Stanislas Haller, BSG

HOW DO I PRAY?

A Little Book of Guidance

JOHN PRITCHARD

Church Publishing
NEW YORK

First published in Great Britain in 2015 by
Society for Promoting Christian Knowledge
36 Causton Street
London SW1P 4ST
www.spck.org.uk

First published in the United States in 2018 by
Church Publishing
19 East 34th Street
New York, NY 10016
www.churchpublishing.org

Cover design by Jennifer Kopec, 2Pug Design
Typeset by Progressive Publishing Services

Library of Congress Cataloging-in-Publication Data

A record of this book is available from the Library of Congress.

ISBN-13: 978-1-64065-031-2 (pbk.)
ISBN-13: 978-1-64065-032-9 (ebook)

Printed in the United States of America

Contents

Introduction

It happens to most of us at some time or other. A faint stirring somewhere that there may be more to this life than meets the eye? The thought just flits across our air-space – 'I wonder . . . is there something else?' Perhaps something really brilliant or really tragic happens, and we're not sure what to do with it. Perhaps we meet someone who really impresses us and we discover that person is a Christian. Or we go into a cathedral and something gently tugs at our subconscious. Maybe it even gets as far as a sense of reaching out from inside ourselves for something. But what? That elusive 'something else'.

Or maybe it even gets as far as a sense of gratitude, a sense of something given. 'Thank God for that,' we say, before we realize what we've said. Because God for many of us is still very much an open question. So it's really rather embarrassing to feel gratitude when we're not sure who to thank. But we fall crazily in love with a person or a place or simply with life itself, and we reach instinctively for someone to thank.

All of these are common human experiences, but we usually don't notice them and they get buried under an avalanche of new experiences surging along behind. These stirrings, however, may be profoundly significant. This tentative 'reaching out' may be like a fragile plant pushing its way through concrete, but it may be the first playful sign of a huge spiritual adventure.

One writer talked about 'signals of transcendence' which litter our everyday experience. And indeed there are things going on all the time, like longing, laughter, falling in love, playing with a child, natural beauty ('breathtaking'), moments in music ('heart-stopping') – all of which take us outside ourselves for a moment. There's something else going on here. I wonder . . . ?

So the first move in the spiritual adventure that I'm here calling 'prayer' is to recognize these moments when something stirs within us and to savour them. Not to let them be flooded and forgotten, but to notice them and hold them, tenderly, just for a while. And for the time being – that's enough! Just recognize those moments for what they are, or might be. Signals of something else. A hint of something good. A glimpse in the night. A scent on the wind. An invitation.

1

Getting started

Making space for God

So there just might be something in it – this 'something else'. And we might have noticed some germ of an instinct, some stirring inside. A reaching out. An instinct to say thank you, a need to say sorry, or a desire to help someone. But we can all too easily lose the moment unless we make space for it to breathe.

And that's what we're terribly short of in our culture – space to let quiet things breathe. The pace of daily life is accelerating and the demands are unremitting. It's as if we got on the 8.15 from Great Snoring, the slow train that stops at every little village, but instead of chugging its way gently through the countryside it gets faster and faster, accelerating steadily and inexorably, steaming through every station, until the carriage is swaying alarmingly and we're hanging on to our seats and to our luggage – and still the speed increases! When is it going to come off the tracks?

Or here's another image. You know when your suitcase is full, and not just full, but absolutely full to bursting? You jam another shirt in and kneel on the case to shut it. And now there's a sweater you'd forgotten. You stand on the case to force it shut. No more, you say! And then you realize you've left out your sponge bag. It's just no use. You can't fit anything else in. You need a different strategy. You need to start again.

In a culture where speed and the ability to 'pack more in' is becoming self-defeating, many people are crying out for space. They long to slow down. A group of porters were once rushing through the jungle at a ridiculous pace set by the Europeans who had hired them. Eventually they got to a clearing and sat down. The Europeans tried to get them moving again but the head porter said, 'No, we're not moving. We've come so far and so fast that now we have to wait for our souls to catch up with us.' So does our culture.

Individually, therefore, we need to build some slowing-down time into our lives. Then we can listen to the quiet whispers from another country that we're just becoming aware of. We need to look for the moments of calm in our day and stretch them out.

We need to create times for stopping, taking everything out of the case and trying a different way of packing altogether. Slowing down is a vital part of the spiritual journey. Then we can stop panicking about when we're going to come off the rails, and start noticing the fascinating countryside we're travelling through.

Imagine a glass of muddy water. When it's shaken up and disturbed the water becomes murky and unpleasant. Let the glass rest, however, and you see the cloudiness in the water gradually clear as the dirt settles to the bottom. Eventually you have clear water and a dark sediment beneath. In some such way, when we slow down, the water of our inner life clears and we're able to see and understand what's really going on inside us. This is the next stage of our spiritual journey.

Talking to God

When we've noticed that there may be 'something else' going on in our lives, and then tried to make some space to stretch out those experiences a bit, there'll come a time when we'll probably want to use words in what we might begin to call 'prayer'.

Words aren't compulsory! It's just that we're speaking animals and we've always entrusted our thoughts and feelings to words in a desire to communicate with each other – and with God.

We live in a society that uses words in vast quantities. We send them everywhere, by letter, fax, e-mail, internet, phone, texts, tweets, blogs, junk mail, and a huge output of newspapers and magazines. We're drowning in words, but rarely is there much judgement or discernment about our use of them. We're simply promiscuous with them.

And yet words are the best tools we've got for communication, so it shouldn't be surprising that our venture into prayer will soon take us into this dangerous arena. We've slowed down in order to give opportunity for those stirrings of thankfulness, wonder or need to see the light of day. We've made space to get in touch with what's going on inside us. Now comes the desire to speak to the 'something else' that seems increasingly like a Someone Else.

But what shall we say?

Three things that don't matter:

1 Quantity

We don't have to say a lot. We just have to say what we want, or what we feel strongly about. In any case, saying a lot may mean we lose the point. Woody

Allen once said, 'I took a speed reading course and read *War and Peace* in twenty minutes. It's about Russia.' Prayer is about life, all of it, but we don't need to talk about it all at once!

2 Quality

We don't have to speak well, in good English, with nicely rounded phrases. Authenticity is what matters. It's a conversation, not an exam.

3 Knowledge

We don't need to have a theology degree to speak to God any more than we need a medical degree to speak to a doctor. Prayer is for amateurs, and we remain amateurs all our lives.

Two things that do matter:

1 Being natural

In the Bible it's said that Moses talked with God 'as with a friend' (Exodus 33.11). That's the model. We simply talk with him about anything and everything, in the sporadic, or focused, or 'um-er' way we talk to anyone in the daily round of our lives. When we talk to God there's no need to put on evening dress.

2 Being honest

A schoolboy was very angry about his parents splitting up, and that anger spilled over on to God.

He heard a sermon about Jacob arguing and fighting with God through the night, so he went back to his room and burst out, 'God, I hate you.' 'Excellent,' said his chaplain, later. Why? Because he was being honest. The psalms are full of the passionate cries of honest people venting their feelings before God. Honesty is what God deals with best.

Becoming aware of God's presence

Prayer is sometimes spoken of as talking with God. But if that's the case, how come we hear so little from God's side? Perhaps we're gaining confidence that we can say things to God, however hesitantly, but the other end of the line seems pretty quiet. And in any case, if people say they hear the voice of God, we tend automatically to wonder about their medical history. So what does 'listening' mean in the context of prayer? And not in a way that requires a PhD in prayer – we're happy to be learning the alphabet here. What does listening to God mean for the beginner or the 'beginner-again'?

Essentially it means being open and attentive to God, who will be wanting to communicate his love to us in many more ways than simply with words. 'Listening' is a bit misleading. Words, or the faculty of hearing, are too narrow as categories. God communicates his presence to us through the whole fabric of life, but nearly always shyly, without attempting to overwhelm us and take away our freedom. God is always coming towards us, at every moment, and in everything that happens. Our task is to be more attentive to his coming, to listen between the lines, to catch the silent music.

Prayer, then, is simply being present to the presence of God, which we can do in a multitude of ways in the midst of life as well as when we give him time and priority. Prayer is being with God, in all sorts of ways and at all sorts of times. And when we're there, so is God. He may be there obviously or very quietly. We may be struck between the eyes or quite unaware of his presence. But he will always be there, gracefully active in the deep places of our lives. And we may become aware of this at any time – when we're putting out the washing, queuing in the supermarket, or listening to a colleague in a meeting. Be attentive – listen – and there'll be something deeper to discover. He may be hidden, but he's not hiding.

It was Woody Allen (again!) who said, 'Eighty per cent of life is just turning up.' So is prayer. Most of it is just turning up and letting God be God. If we're aware of him – great. If we're not – fine. He's still at work with us. He's got plenty of time, and he's a wonderful opportunist! Whatever we give him, he's always saying, 'Now what shall we make of this?'

But let's be particular. 'Listening' isn't about hearing voices; it's a much bigger attentiveness to a God who is always coming towards us at every moment. God always starts the conversation because he's always reaching out to us.

But how will we notice his presence?

- Sometimes we might be aware of 'deep thoughts' – ideas and convictions which formulate themselves as we pause and pray. Listen to them, because they've at last been able to surface, and God may be in them. If so, they will have their own authenticity. We'll recognize their truth.

- Sometimes that moment of recognition will come through what others say, or what we read or see, or through events themselves, and we'll recognize the force of that insight as being for us. It drives home. It has the ring of truth about it. It may not strike anyone else; it's a personal 'disclosure'. It's God dealing with our heart.

- God often speaks to people through the language of creation. His world is just so stunningly beautiful, in the smallest detail or in the grandest sweep. Grown men are brought to tears by sunset in the Himalayas or left speechless by the incredible colours of the fish in the Gulf of Aqaba. Nature constantly amazes us and invites us to respond.

- Very often God will communicate through his special Word, the Bible. Here is the wisdom of God, actively seeking us out. In the interaction between this Book of Books and the deep places of our hearts God communicates through the electric charge of the Spirit. Sometimes we'll be stopped in our tracks; sometimes we'll be challenged to the core; sometimes we'll be made aware of his incredible love. Our task is to listen to our hearts as we read the transcript of God's love.

- Another form of encounter with this God who is constantly coming towards us is through what may be a deep emotional response to music, or poetry, or a book or film, or someone relating an incident in their lives. From deep within comes a profound set of unexpected emotions with the divine signature discreetly upon them.

Relating to God

Prayer is about exploring a relationship with God, not about perfecting an esoteric technique. It may help, therefore, to use an image of prayer like another deep relationship – that between husband and wife. If a marriage is to be healthy the relationship needs to exist at four levels:

1 *'Just getting on with it'.* Much of marriage is lived naturally and unselfconsciously. We don't go on about it; we just live with that relationship as a backdrop. Similarly much of our relationship with God involves simply getting on with the pleasures and problems of living, but doing that against the background of God's good presence. And all of us can grin at God occasionally!

2 *Chatting.* An essential part of marriage is the daily sharing of a hundred minor conversations about nothing much at all. 'Do remember that dental appointment, won't you?' 'Could you get to the bank for me today?' 'I thought you were going to change that Damien Hirst poster in the kitchen?' Similarly, much of our day-to-day communication with God will be by chatting – what we call 'arrow prayers', i.e. quick-contact, instant-access prayers.

3 *Talking.* Any marriage needs proper conversation that gets down to things that matter. There may not be a lot of time in any one day, but thoughts, feelings, deeper things, need to come out and be shared. So with God. We need at some time to have the space and the focus of simply being with God, to deepen the relationship. This is where the going gets tough!

4 *Intimacy.* Marriage partners need to remain 'in touch' with each other – literally. They need to go beyond words to actions and the world of the senses. This is where touch, love and intimate silence have their place. In prayer too there is a time when words fall away and silence, meditation and the simple enjoyment of God take over.

Use the checklist above on levels of relationship and apply it to your relationship with God. Do you want to adjust your own way of praying in any way yet? Or will you just keep this checklist in mind for future use?

Finding a special time for prayer

We've looked at 'just getting on with it' prayer and 'chatting' prayer in the last section. What we come to look at now is 'talking' prayer, what to do in the time we've set aside especially to focus on our relationship with God. Without some such dedicated time that relationship is likely to suffer as much as a human relationship that isn't valued properly or given enough time and attention. It may not be possible to find that time every day, but it has to be found on some days or we'll notice the difference. The concert pianist Artur Rubinstein once said: 'If I don't practise for a day, I notice the difference; if I don't practise for two days, my family notices the difference; if I don't practise for three days, the public notices the difference.'

When? The most important thing here is regularity. It doesn't matter when the time is, as long as it's regular. Depending on our life-situation, it could be early in the morning (there are such people, I'm told), in the commuter train, after getting the children off to school, during a lunch break in a park or a city church, after supper if we're not going out, or maybe last thing at night. For a student it could be when you first get to your desk. For other people it could be when walking the dog, or cooking, or even changing the baby's nappy. (Be gentle with yourself if you have a young family – it's the most difficult time of all to sustain a life of prayer.) We have to be flexible in our timing but this period of prayer needs to become a regular part of our life rather than an extra we might easily forget.

Where? What we need here is somewhere that becomes associated with prayer, so that simply to go to that place takes us halfway into the presence of God already. The particular place may be a chair by the window or in the kitchen; it may be a corner of a room, set up to be a special 'chapel'; it may even be a seat on the train or in the car, or a particular part of a walk. Places are more significant than many people think. We all of us have special places – be they football grounds, the setting of a first romance, the scene of a glorious holiday. And sacred places, too, matter very much – places where heaven has opened a crack, where an angel's wing has brushed our face, or where we've experienced mystery. There are no rules about where our special place should be, at home, in a church or in a field. But when you get there – stay. The philosopher Pascal said: 'Most of the troubles of man come from him not being able to stay alone in his own room.' In other words, there is serious business to be done here – don't run away.

With what things? If we are going to have our own space at home then a number of questions arise about what we'll need with us. Again, this is very much up to personal choice. Many of us value having a cross at the centre of our vision, or an icon. Candles speak a common language and lighting a candle marks out the time we're giving to this special purpose of prayer. Something of beauty may help – flowers are common. We may also have a small CD player or iPod to play appropriate music as we settle in. A simple prayer stool where you tuck your legs under the cross-piece is comfortable and relaxed. And of course we need the Bible with us, and maybe a few other devotional books to help our prayer and reflection. This is a place to be at home in, so the choices we make are very personal. In the centre of my own sacred space, under the cross, is a pair of pottery hands I got on the Greek island of Patmos. These open hands are a constant symbol of my need to open myself to God, and also to place in his hands the needs and issues of the day.

Starting the day with God

Drive down any street in Britain today and you see a forest of little black satellite dishes turning their eager faces towards the skies. They represent a huge amount of enjoyment funnelling into those homes – and maybe a tiny bit of wasted time! In my imagination I'd like to think that all over the country at the start of the day there are even more minds and hearts turning towards God, like human satellite dishes, open to receive all the good things he has for us.

As soon as our feet hit the carpet in the morning we're on the go. Familiar routines slot into place. People flit in and out of bathrooms, bedrooms and kitchens by some unspoken, sophisticated choreography. A small variation in the expected moves ('Martin, will you please get up **now**!') causes a major breakdown in the system. Breakfast is a time of clipped conversation about marmalade, tetchy reminders about sports kit, and the dog always being in the wrong place, all to the background of an argument about politics on the radio. So where does prayer fit into this lot?

The key is regularity. It doesn't matter whether our way of starting the day with God is a snatched greeting or an extended conversation – the important thing is that it becomes part of the choreography of the morning. We don't have to think each morning about whether we're going to clean our teeth or not, because it's part of the routine. We just do it, without agonizing, and we know we're the better for it. So with prayer.

There's a short way and a long way to start the day with God. With a young family or an early start we'll probably simply want to place the day in God's hands and then get on with it. If the day is our own or we're retired we might want to make this the main time of prayer and spiritual input. But then again, temperament comes into it. Some of us like to settle into a longer, reflective time with God, while that drives others of us to chew the dog basket. Horses for courses; patterns for people.

So we may find it best to pray briefly by the washbasin while cleaning our teeth, or while walking the dog, or while commuting to work. Alternatively we might have fifteen minutes in the kitchen before anyone else comes down, or a relaxed time after breakfast when everything is quiet. The important principle is to make the time a regular one, and in it to place all the day – its events, its conversations, its work, its emotions – into God's safe hands. Then whatever happens in the day, we know he's there.

And all we've had to do is switch on the satellite receiver.

Ending the day with God

So we've got to the end of the day! The pace slackens; darkness falls. It's like a car slowing down as it comes off the motorway, or a ship nosing its way into port. We're 'coming home' at the end of the day.

For many people this is a good time to pray because there's plenty of 'stuff' to pray about. In particular this is a good time to review the day, to see it in the light of God, and so perhaps to grow in personal and spiritual awareness. By looking back on the day, thoughtfully and prayerfully, we might become more aware of God's footprints through the day, and we might even come to know ourselves a little better.

The crucial activity is *reflection*, which is simply looking at the past and trying to learn from it. Ronald Knox, a translator of the Bible, was a very precocious child, and he often couldn't get to sleep at night. When he was four years old his parents asked him what he did when he couldn't sleep and he answered, with all the seriousness and experience of his four years, 'I lie there and I think about the past.' At least he had the right idea! Someone said, 'The unreflected life is not worth living.' That may be a bit extreme, but the point is well made that thinking through what we have experienced is a huge resource for living in the future.

Living a life of prayer

There was a book which came out in 1963 called *Prayers of Life* by a French priest named Michel Quoist. It blew like a gale through the staid vocabulary of a lot of conventional prayer, largely because it refused to recognize any human experience as off-limits to prayer. So there are prayers over a five-pound note, a wire fence, a tractor, football at night – even a bald head! One section of the book is headed 'All of life would become prayer', and the phrase has always stuck in my mind as the final goal of all this activity we call prayer – not that all of life should be made up of religious piety, but that all of life should be gently lived before God.

Margaret Silf, in the final chapter of her book *Taste and See*, uses the illustration of a birdwatcher who sometimes goes into his hide, but who actually learns to listen to the birds all the time, not just when he goes into his special place. The birdwatcher gradually becomes tuned in to the birds *permanently*, even when he's not in his hide, and he notices all the patterns in the songs and the subtle changes in modulation and pitch, and indeed the whole panorama of sound which the rest of us usually screen out.

So our special times of prayer, our times in the 'hide', help us to tune in to the fullness of God's voice which is constantly with us, but is usually unheard against the background hiss of modern life. There is a place for effort in prayer, but the ultimate goal is that all of life should become prayer, lived thankfully in the presence of God.

When a human life is entirely pervaded by the presence and love of another person, he or she experiences life as a limitless possibility. Life is breathtakingly beautiful, and obstacles are there to be leapt over. So if a human life is entirely pervaded by the presence and love of God, who knows what might happen? It will certainly be good – very good. All of life will become wrapped up in the light and tenderness of God. All of life will become prayer.

2

Going deeper

Soaking in the silence

For many people there comes a time in their spiritual journey where they find themselves longing for more silence. They find a small pool of silence in the midst of a busy day and they jump in fully clothed. Silence is so rare, and yet for many people today it's like a deep thirst.

Just as this page you're reading needs both black print and white paper in order for us to communicate, so in prayer we need both the 'black space' of words and the 'white space' of silence. Silence provides the context in which words may or may not be necessary. We sometimes need to soundproof the heart in order to hear the whisper of God in a noisy world.

Silence seems to be pretty important to God. The birth of Jesus took place in the silence of a stable at night. The death of Jesus took place in the silence and darkness of a cross. The resurrection of Jesus took place in the silence before the dawn. Three huge events that took place in silence.

So we shouldn't be surprised that some of the deepest exchanges between us and God may take place in silence. If we have felt ourselves drawn to explore silence we'll need a quiet place and sufficient time. We may only start with five or ten minutes, and even that may seem agonizingly long at first, but the golden rule is 'don't panic!' Stay in there and soon that time will seem hopelessly short. It may still be difficult to stay focused, but that time will become an essential spiritual bath in which to soak and be refreshed.

Taking the water image further, what we are trying to do in silent prayer is a bit like getting under the surface of the sea where, a few feet beneath the turbulence of the waves, is a gentle stillness. Like the waves in a stormy sea, our lives may be frenetic on the surface, but underneath we may be able to enter a realm of mental and spiritual peace where our agitations are resolved and God is able to steal into our lives.

In this kind of prayer we aren't trying to *achieve* anything. There's nothing to 'get through'. We simply open ourselves to God and wait. Certainly there are things to help us, but the essence of it is the waiting on God, listening to the silent thunder of the Lord of glory. Many times we'll walk away and not be sure what happened, if anything. But that's fine. It's the same with most evening meals in my life – I don't remember precisely what I ate last week, let alone ten years ago. But without them, and without silent prayer, my life and health would be infinitely poorer!

Entering the mystery

Praying in silence may lead us into still deeper waters. We start with a verse or an image to take us into silence and to act as a touchstone if we get lost, but eventually we may find that we actually enjoy being lost! Silence can become addictive!

What we're getting into now is classically called 'contemplation'. Instead of thinking or praying with words, we now cut down our actions simply to looking; we look towards God. The nearest description, perhaps, is 'gazing'. When we look at a work of art, or at someone we love, it isn't sufficient just to glance fleetingly in that direction; we need to gaze at the image before us in order to be open to all that it (or he or she) has to offer. The delight is in the looking. Small children do this naturally. You see them completely absorbed by a few shells on a beach, or the sand running through their hands. But when they grow up . . .

Contemplation is about giving attention to God. We live in a culture which neurotically encourages us to give attention to ourselves, leading us to believe that with a little more self-absorption and self-help we can achieve The Answers To All Life's Problems. In that context contemplation seems so counter-cultural as to be verging on quaint. But it also strikes many people as being hugely refreshing. It points us out of our self-preoccupation and towards the crisp fresh air and the stunning beauty of the Lord of Hosts.

Our society needs contemplatives because it needs people who can 'see'. It needs contemplative *places* because that's where the atmosphere is thinner and the world of the Spirit more visible. It needs contemplative *communities* because that's where people pray steadily, look steadily and live steadily – all in the direction of God.

But we too can experience contemplative prayer.

Having said that, the way to enter the mystery beyond words and images is one of the most difficult moves to describe in the whole life of prayer. How do you teach people to fall in love? They either do or they don't. But the place to start is in that silent centring, focusing and waiting described in the previous section.

We may then find that we need words and images less; they become a bit of a blur. What we find ourselves doing is simply being with God, gazing in his direction. And that's sufficient. It may be comfortable; it may be dark and dreary. It may be wonder-full or a trackless desert. No matter: the point is to *be there*, and simply to let God be God for once.

There are no rules in this form of prayer, and nothing to achieve. So don't go there unless you are inexorably drawn to do so. Don't imagine that contemplation is spiritually romantic and something to slip into the next conversation with the vicar. This prayer isn't for romantics; it's for mystics.

Making it through the wilderness

Sometimes prayer is simply boring. We don't like to admit that. Indeed, Christians have a vested interest in making it seem that their faith is successful and enjoyable, and that it works. It's understandable. Why else should anyone want to become a Christian if it doesn't work? But nevertheless, sometimes it all seems meaningless and dry. We've run out of energy. The tank is empty.

If you ask people why they are Christians you might get answers like, 'Because it gives my life meaning,' 'Because it works,' 'Because it's true.' But you then have to ask the questions: What happens when that faith doesn't make sense of what's going on in your life? What happens when it doesn't seem to work? What happens when serious doubts begin to assail the mind and gnaw away at the heart? Because they will.

Consider the experience of one leading spiritual writer, Henri Nouwen, whose books and teaching have inspired millions.

> So what about my life of prayer? Do I like to pray? Do I want to pray? Do I spend time praying? Frankly, the answer is no to all three questions. After sixty-three years of life and thirty-eight years of priesthood, my prayer seems as dead as a rock . . . I have paid much attention to prayer, reading about it, writing about it, visiting monasteries, and guiding many people on their spiritual journeys. By now I should be full of spiritual fire, consumed by prayer. Many people think I am and speak to me as if prayer is my greatest gift and deepest desire.
>
> The truth is that I do not feel much, if anything, when I pray. There are no warm emotions, bodily sensations, or mental visions. None of my five senses is being

touched – no special smells, no special sounds, no special sights, no special tastes, and no special movements. Whereas for a long time the Spirit acted so clearly through my flesh, now I feel nothing. I have lived with the expectation that prayer would become easier as I grow older and closer to death. But the opposite seems to be happening. The words 'darkness' and 'dryness' seem best to describe my prayer today . . .

Are the darkness and dryness of my prayer signs of God's absence, or are they signs of a presence deeper and wider than my senses can contain? Is the death of my prayer the end of my intimacy with God or the beginning of a new communion, beyond words, emotions, and bodily sensations?

Henri Nouwen, *Sabbatical Journey*
(London, Darton, Longman & Todd, 2013)

Unfortunately we can't answer that last question because a few months later Nouwen was dead. But it's a vital question for many people because it's part of a larger question: is this experience of dryness just a particular passing phase due to all sorts of other factors, or is it a major stage in my spiritual journey?

There's an important divide here. Much spiritual dryness is due to external factors. Maybe we've been on the Christian road a long time and are just travel weary. Maybe we're tired and stressed in other areas of life and so, of course, our spiritual life reflects that. Or maybe we've got stuck in a set of practices of worship and prayer that we've outgrown and we need a new wardrobe. There are all sorts of reasons.

But there's another experience altogether that starts out looking the same – boredom, listlessness, dryness – but is actually what has often been called 'the dark night of the soul' or senses. This is the experience when, as Henri Nouwen wonders, we are being moved on by God to a profounder union with the divine where we are too close to the light to see it. St John of the Cross explained it by saying that the clearer the light shines, the more it blinds and darkens the eye of the soul. The eye of the soul dilates, and faith becomes trust in the unseen God. If the experience of darkness is of this sort then God is in charge and he is teaching the Christian not to rely on the senses but on God alone. It's a stage of growth.

But if it's the other sort of darkness where we've run our truck into the desert and got stuck in the sand, then there will be things we ourselves could be doing about it. The question we are then being asked is like the question asked by the group leader in the mountains after his party has collapsed on the ground for a break: 'Shall we move on?' he asks optimistically. If we don't get up and move on with the main party, all we can do is dawdle ineffectually down the mountain, but if we're ready to move on there's new territory to explore and new height to be gained. And that's what this section is about – hearing the question 'Shall we move on?' and answering, 'Yes.'

Preparing for action

A theological student once took an old Bible and a pair of scissors and cut out of the Bible every reference to the poor, or God's concern for the marginalized, or God's demand for justice for the oppressed. It took him a very long time but when he'd finished, the Bible literally fell apart. It was a Bible full of holes.

Some people who have read this far may be getting impatient. It may seem to them that prayer is an activity too cut off from the risks and struggles of ordinary life. It may even seem as if prayer is an escape into a pink mist of personal spirituality, where the consolations of the inner life substitute for the harder realities of twenty-first-century living.

Contrast this with the words of theologian Kenneth Leech. 'True spirituality is not a leisure-time activity, a diversion from life. It is essentially subversive, and the test of its genuineness is practical.' Or the famous theologian Karl Barth: 'To clasp the hands in prayer is the beginning of an uprising against the disorder of the world.' There must be a direct link between how we pray and how we act. It isn't sufficient to pray away happily in our own quiet spaces without engaging with the needs and the pain of society.

The reason for this is clear. Contact with the living God is bound to propel us into action, just as the relationship of Jesus with his heavenly Father propelled him into healing the unhealed, touching the untouchable, and meeting the marginalized on their own ground. His message wasn't about self-fulfilment, self-actualization or any other self-centred therapy; it was about a kingdom of justice, mercy and peace. He declared that this kingdom of God was breaking in, there and then, and he challenged people to join up to that great project. He didn't come with a spiritual duvet but with a spiritual alarm-clock.

What does this mean for prayer?

• You could pray about world issues, straight from the news. Use your imagination to envisage the human cost. Struggle with God and with yourself if you find points of resistance and confusion as you pray.

Like Jacob struggling with the divine stranger through the night, don't let go!

- Listen to the niggling voice in your heart that tells you to get on and do something about some of these things you see and hear of. Let the environmental crisis get you involved with Friends of the Earth; let the rough sleepers in your city get you involved with a night shelter; let a friend in despair lead you to go on a listening course.

- See prayer as a dangerous activity. Peace worker Daniel Berrigan: 'The time will shortly be upon us, if it is not already here, when the pursuit of contemplation becomes a strictly subversive activity.' Martin Luther King talked about Christians needing to be 'creatively maladjusted' to the prevailing norms of society. The reason is that true prayer purifies the mind and heart of the layers of self-deception which become caked over the soul. Prayer should strip down our spiritual lives to basics, and there we might discover the resources to resist injustice.

- Determine that when you pray for someone in need that you will also ask the question, 'And is there something I could do to be part of answering my own prayer?' It may be sending a card assuring them of your love and prayer; it may be making a meal for a stressed family; it may be going and taking their ironing away, or just going and listening. There may not be much you can actually do in some situations, but ask the question anyway.

- When you read the life of Jesus in the Gospels, read it in the light of the central gospel proclamation, 'The kingdom of God is at hand.' If you can recognize the social and political challenge inherent in those words it will enliven your reading of the Gospels and your appreciation of the threat Jesus posed. This Jesus was dangerous, and his followers today should have something of that same whiff of danger about them!

Praying for others

I wonder how many requests God receives in an average day? It will certainly run into hundreds of millions. Cyberspace is constantly packed with prayer, delivered to that well-known address <www.Jesus .com>. Christians call this praying for others 'intercession', and it's the most common form of prayer. Indeed, it's what many people think you mean when you talk about prayer – forgetting all the other prayer such as giving thanks, being sorry, and silently resting in God.

But that's fine with God. He takes whatever we offer and works with it, and if we come with a list of requests, he might well say: 'Fair enough. it's what Jesus told them to do. Ask and you'll receive, seek and you'll find, knock and the door will fly open' (Luke 11.9). Sometimes, of course, we do rather take advantage of that promise. An eighteenth-century businessman prayed like this: 'O Lord, who knowest I have mine estates in the City of London, and likewise that I have lately purchased an estate in the county of Essex, I beseech thee to preserve the two counties of Middlesex and Essex from fire and earthquake. For the rest of the counties thou mayest deal with them as thou art pleased.'

Fortunately God isn't proud and he takes all our prayers and uses them, sometimes having to work quite hard to pull them round to make some sort of sense! He may have to answer the deeper prayer rather than the superficial one we actually put to him. He may have to resist the role of magician. But he still honours and uses our deep instinct to pray.

When we pray for others what makes it so special is that it's a way of loving them. It's the best and biggest thing we can do for anyone, to hold them before God and expose them to the power of love, the power which, after all, makes and sustains the world. So saying that we'll pray for someone is a serious commitment to loving that person enough to take them regularly to God. It isn't a spiritual sticking plaster to enable us to make a clean getaway.

The basis of our prayer for other people is that fundamentally we all belong to one another, so 'if one part of the body suffers, all suffer together with it' (1 Corinthians 12.26). If you think of the earth's crust without any oceans, all parts of the world are joined. As John Donne wrote: 'No man is an island, entire of itself; every man is a piece of the continent, a part of the main.' So we are joined, we belong, and that makes intercession both natural for us to offer, and possible for God to use.

But I'd like to raise the stakes a bit and suggest that prayer for the world, and for others in it, is no less than joining in God's majestic project to transform the world. It isn't about finding lost car keys or curing Aunt Mabel's ingrowing toenail. It's making ourselves part of God's massive attack on evil and on everything that destroys, distorts or cramps human life. Wherever Jesus found evil in his ministry he opposed it, and he invited his disciples (and all Rabbit's friends and relations) to join in the campaign. It was a campaign of love, and by our prayer we can be part of that campaign now.

3

Keeping moving

Isn't prayer a rather infantile activity?

'I mean, you grow out of it, don't you? It's nice to believe in a friendly face behind the clouds when you're young, but in the real world you make your own luck. It's tough out there and you've got to be tough yourself if you're going to survive. Prayer belongs to junior school.'

There are three things to say to all that. In the first place, it's not infantile to pray to God if in fact the human heart is made for him, if the deepest reality of our being is that we are constantly searching for our spiritual home. People of faith maintain that our deepest selves need to 'dock' with God if we are to grow towards wholeness. Prayer then becomes a sign of maturity, not of childishness.

Second, prayer can certainly be infantile if as adults we still pray in infantile ways. The fresh faith of a child can be truly delightful. Remember the prayer of a child overheard by his mother: 'Dear God, please look after Mum and Dad, and Stephen, and Grandma and Granddad, and Aunty Clare and Uncle Mark, and our dog Spot, and please look after yourself, because if you don't do that, we're all sunk!' But we grow into more thoughtful and considered forms of prayer as we grow older and more experienced in faith. Prayer may become more reflective and our requests more nuanced. Just as other relationships mature, so will our relationship with God in prayer.

Third, there's a difference between being *childish* and being *childlike*. It's not appropriate to pray in child*ish* ways when we are adults. To pray that my Lottery number will come up isn't likely to persuade the celestial civil service! It isn't really on (though it's entirely understandable) to pray as the woman did when she'd dropped a whole tray of crockery: 'Dear God, may that not just have happened!' But it certainly is appropriate for us to pray with the child*like* trust of one who knows their heavenly Father to be entirely good, compassionate and true. That's why Jesus told us that when we pray we should call God *Abba* – Dad.

How can we pray meaningfully when we live in a universe governed by scientific laws?

Well, let's clear the ground a bit here. So-called 'scientific laws' are in fact only the regularities we observe in nature. They're not written in cosmic stone. These regularities are of course essential to us. We need to know that jumping off a cliff will have certain negative consequences. But the natural world is much more 'open-textured' than our limited understanding supposes. Scientists tell us that the deepest level of reality we can understand thus far isn't at all solid but is made up of a swirling mass of string-like energy. We know that the universe isn't predictable in the normal understanding of the word, but is built up of a subtle interplay of chance and necessity.

When we pray, therefore, we aren't throwing paper darts at some iron wall of natural law. We're co-operating with God in his massive enterprise of healing creation, bit by bit. When I pray I'm not asking God to interrupt the ordinary workings of the universe. I'm asking him to work within the created order of things so that the full potential and capacity of that part of creation may be released. I'm looking for the natural order to be at full stretch, just as it was in Jesus (which is why amazing things happened around him).

This approach to prayer therefore sees God not as *over*-ruling anything so much as *under*-ruling it. He rules from *within* his created order. God's action isn't a violation of 'natural law'; rather, it is itself the natural law of a deeper order of reality, what happens when we break through to the deepest levels of nature's operation.

Prayer then becomes an exciting cooperation with the One who holds everything in being. God doesn't have to squeeze into his world like a child trying to get into his parents' dinner party. It *is* his world and he wants to share its joys and responsibilities with us. In prayer we work at it together.

What about prayer that never gets answered?

What indeed! Who of us hasn't got a few questions to ask God when we get to meet him? What about the floods and famines we prayed about, the weeping by the bedside, the desperate praying for a wounded marriage? What more does this God want, to get him into action?

Well, if we remember the last question about a scientific universe we'll realize that God is both free and limited within the fabric of his creation. He has limited himself in the interests of love. He has tied his hands behind his back in the very act of creating a universe in order that it should have the freedom to be itself. It happens in any human act of creation, too. When we 'create' children (without going into details!) we limit our freedom over them. They have an independent existence which means that we can thereafter persuade, advise or cajole our children, but we can't enforce anything ultimately, except in the most meaningless sense. John V. Taylor once wrote: 'The truth about God is not so much that he is omnipotent as that he is inexhaustible, and for that reason he will always succeed.' But 'success' may not be as we know it!

Two people I know and care for have cancer as I write. I'm praying for them both but I know that the course of their illness will inevitably be different. What if one has a marvellous remission and the other dies rapidly? What will I say about the use of my prayer or the trustworthiness of God? What I hope I'll do is realize that God is absolutely committed to both these people and wills the very best for both of them. Indeed, he will be working flat out, within the givens of the situation, for the welfare and wholeness of both. But what I also hope I'll accept is that there are intrinsic limitations to those 'givens', and I don't know what

God. Prayer is holding open the door of opportunity in places of despair. Prayer is struggle, joy, laughter and pain. In other words, prayer doesn't have to be a spiritual massage, a scent of roses and a warm glow. It's too important for that.

What matters more than how we feel is what we bring. If we bring ourselves and the people on our hearts then we'll be entering the arena of prayer with honesty and love. What happens then is God's business. If we're taken off to the seventh heaven – wonderful (and sometimes it will happen). If we're left cleaning up the spiritual garbage – thanks be to God (someone had to do it). Some of us are more emotional than others and God works with us as he finds us. Faithfulness matters more than feelings.

On the other hand, it's important that prayer doesn't remain at the level of duty and determination all the time. As the psychotherapist Carl Jung said, 'It is of the highest importance that people should know religious truth as a thing living in the human soul, and not as an abstruse and unreasonable relic of the past.' Prayer has to permeate the heart. Nevertheless, that permeating can be done through inner conviction as well as through feelings. Different people will experience prayer in different ways, and long live the difference!

How can prayer be kept fresh?

Prayer is a long-term relationship, not a one-night stand. It therefore has its moments when you say to yourself: 'Whose clever idea was this, then?' There aren't many days when we wake up thinking, 'Oh, what a beautiful morning – can't wait to pray!' We're not talking here about the spiritual wilderness we talked about in Chapter 2, just the ordinariness of much of the spiritual journey.

A lot of the road to heaven has to be taken at 30 miles an hour. Occasionally we get on to a stretch of motorway and take off, but more often we have to go through the built-up areas, the road works and the general snarl-up of life – and in the middle of all that, to keep reasonably fresh at the wheel.

It might be helpful every so often to do a kind of spiritual audit and ask ourselves these sorts of questions:

- Does the word 'prayer' feel warm or cold to you at present?
- On a scale of 1 to 10, how well do you feel you are doing in keeping prayerfully in touch with God?
- What's at the heart of your prayer life right now?

- Do your inner and outer lives feel in touch with each other at the moment?
- What levels or types of prayer do you seem to be using these days? (See Chapter 1)

   'Just getting on with it' (but remembering God is there)?

   Chatting (quick-contact, 'instant access' prayer)?

   Talking (time set apart for the purpose)?

   Intimacy (going beyond words)?

- If you were to think of yourself as a 'praying animal', what animal would you be? And why? A small black and white mongrel, well-meaning but insecure? A brown bear, crashing about in the forest in a rather ungainly fashion? A kitten, curled up in his Master's lap but sometimes stuck up a tree!?

The answers to these questions may be encouraging or dispiriting. The point is not to get stressed about it but to realize that prayer to God has the full range of experiences and emotions which we know in any important relationship. The task is to keep our prayer and life of faith as fresh as possible without expecting always to be living on the spiritual equivalent of cloud nine.

A lifetime's journey

The time has come for the real journey to begin. This book has tried to offer a whole range of useful items to put in the rucksack, but only you can make the journey. When our daughter set off for her gap year in Africa, everything she needed for a year had to go into one rucksack, and as parents we worked hard with her to make sure she had the right things. But one morning she went through the airport departure gate alone.

The adventure of prayer is more than a year; it's a lifetime journey into God, and into the high mountains of the spirit. Although the journey is ours and no one can make it for us, nevertheless we can take a rucksack full of good things and, more importantly, we'll be travelling with the very best Guide there is – Jesus Christ himself, who promised to be with us always, to the end of all time (Matthew 28.20). That's a high level of security!

But before we can set out on any significant journey – for instance, marriage, or a career – we need to have a pretty reasonable level of self-knowledge and self-awareness, or we might just come unstuck a little way down the track. So too in the spiritual journey it's important to have some self-knowledge so that we know in broad terms what helps us spiritually, where we can go to find nourishment.

Because human personality is so astonishingly diverse, it shouldn't be a surprise that we have different types of spirituality as well. Throughout this book there will have been things that have attracted you and other things that have elicited little more than a slightly bored 'ho-hum'. So it might now help to consider what kind of spiritual 'personality' you have, and where you can find your daily bread – or caviar.

I've found it useful to adapt a scheme of the nineteenth-century philosopher Friedrich von Hügel who wrote about various 'schools of prayer', represented by particular biblical characters. The point about the brief descriptions that follow is not to try and find a perfect match or expect only to resonate with one or other of the 'schools'. The point is to recognize one (or two) schools which feel to be some sort of spiritual home, while probably finding attractive some part of each of the schools. Knowing our 'home' can give us confidence in our own spiritual journey and prevent us from being threatened by the strange spiritual passions of other people.

School of St Peter This form of spirituality shares some of the robust, 'get-on-with-it' characteristics we associate with Jesus' forthright, red-blooded friend Peter. If this is your spiritual home, you probably pray best in set forms with a recognizable structure, maybe using books of prayers to help. You're likely to be a concrete thinker, attracted to regular worship in church and the unfolding drama of the Church's year, particularly in Holy Week and Easter. You will be loyal and faithful in prayer (at least in intention!) and may value a rule of life or a spiritual friend. Holy Communion may be important to you, but you're more concerned with good, well-prepared and well-led worship. Among the Gospels, Mark may be your favourite.

School of St Paul Paul was the thinker of the early Church, a passionate and intelligent man with a drive to perfectionism. If you pray in this school, you will be thoughtful about prayer and worship, wanting it to make intellectual sense, to be anchored in scripture and to be related to the public world, not just to personal experience. You will probably be a regular reader of spiritual books and a lively critic of sermons! You will be less attracted to what you see as superficial emotion in worship but are actually capable yourself of a deep, passionate response to God; there may be something of the mystic in you. Intercessions should be about the real world and things that matter, not just fluffy personal issues. Among the Gospels you may be drawn to Matthew or to John.

School of St John Tradition has it that John not only had a special friendship with Jesus, he also had many years to ruminate on the events of Jesus' life and death, and these profound reflections are the core of John's Gospel. It's that reflective quality that marks this type of prayer. Prayer is more of a seeking and a reaching out, a longing. It's more opaque and more exploratory. Prayer needs time and space because essentially it's about entering a mystery, not getting a result. You may use few words but value silence, symbols, imagination, poetry. You may prefer a quiet early morning service to the mid-morning all-age jamboree, and you may be rather impatient with what you perceive as superficial prayer and worship which doesn't attend to depth and mystery. Intercession may be your least favoured form of prayer but you respond to imaginative new methods. John's Gospel has to be the one you prefer.

School of St Francis Francis is the popular saint of today because of his obvious love of nature and of ordinary people, and because he was a man of integrity and bold action, giving to the poor and living himself with great simplicity. Perhaps people forget how incredibly demanding his standards were. However, if you belong to his school of prayer you'll find inspiration for prayer in God's creation and in the joys and sufferings of his people. Thanksgiving will come readily to your lips, and you'll identify strongly with people in need, praying for them with deep commitment. Your idealism will be hurt by conflicts among God's people and you'll then find inspiration in the reconciling death and abundant new life of Jesus Christ. You will probably be found putting personal action behind your prayers; you get involved, often at great cost to yourself. You find fellow feeling with Luke's Gospel where women, the poor and the sick are especially in evidence.

The important thing about these 'schools of prayer', remember, is that they merely offer you a home base, a place to recognize as your natural preference. They aren't meant to box you in but rather to give you an approximate description of where you feel most comfortable, so that you can go on your way rejoicing, and picking up as many good gifts from other ways of praying as you can. If you know where home is, you can relax.

This journey is for a lifetime. The rucksack is as large as you want, but it's always light. The Guide of guides is at your side. The way is open before you. So the vital thing now is to get moving and to keep moving.

If you can't fly, run. If you can't run, walk. If you can't walk, crawl. But by all means – keep moving.

Martin Luther King

Further reading

Here is a short list of books that can guide you further in your exploration of the topics discussed in this book.

The text of *How Do I Pray?* is drawn from chapters 1–4, 6, 8–10, 17, 18 and 22–5 of the author's *How To Pray: A Practical Handbook* (London, SPCK 2002).

For more information on that book visit: <www.spckpublishing.co.uk/shop/how-to-pray/>.

Other books of related interest:

All Desires Known, Janet Morley, London, SPCK, 1992. Imaginative, evocative images often with a haunting beauty.

An Anglican Companion, Alan Wilkinson and Christopher Cocksworth (eds), London, SPCK, 2014. Some of the classic prayers and sources of Anglican spirituality.

Approaches to Prayer, Henry Morgan (ed.), London, SPCK, 1991. Full of useful ideas.

God of Surprises, Gerard Hughes, London, Darton, Longman & Todd, 1985. Links the inner journey with the needs of a just society to produce one of the great contemporary books of spiritual guidance.

How to Pray: Alone, With Others, At Any Time, In Any Place, Stephen Cottrell, London, Church House Publishing, 2010. This is a practical and accessible book on how to relate all of life to prayer.

The Intercessions Handbook, John Pritchard, London, SPCK, 1997. Creative ideas for public prayer, prayer groups and personal prayer.

Just As I Am, Ruth Etchells, London, Triangle, 1994. A rich companion of personal prayers to make your own at the beginning and end of the day.

The Lion Prayer Collection, Mary Batchelor (ed.), London, Lion, 1996. Another beautifully produced and comprehensive book of prayers in different styles.

Prayer, Richard Foster, London, Hodder & Stoughton, 1992. A solid way into prayer from a popular and clear writer.

Praying With the Bible, Philip Law, London, SPCK, 2007. A book of prayers drawn from and based on passages of the Bible, with practical suggestions for how they can enrich your prayer life.

Prayers to Remember, Colin Podmore (ed.), London, Darton, Longman & Todd, 2001. As it says – some of the best.

Sadhana: A Way to God, Anthony de Mello, Garden City, NY, Doubleday/Image, 1984. Christian exercises in meditation and silence using both western and eastern forms.

The SPCK Book of Christian Prayer, London, SPCK, 2009. An imaginative, reliable and comprehensive collection of prayers from different Christian traditions.

Spirituality Workbook, David Runcorn, London, SPCK, 2011. A helpful guidebook for seekers and explorers who want their spiritual life to go deeper.

Taste and See, Margaret Silf, London, Darton, Longman & Todd, 1999. An accessible introduction to many forms of prayer, particularly ones using the imagination.

This Sunrise of Wonder, Michael Mayne, London, Fount, 1995. An inventory of joy, leading us to re-examine the importance of wonder in our lives.

Tides and Seasons, David Adam, London, SPCK, 2010. One of the writer's excellent books drawing on the Celtic tradition of prayer. See also *The Open Gate*, London, SPCK, 2006.

Too Busy Not to Pray, Bill Hybels, Downers Grove, IL, Inter-Varsity Press, 1998. Practical and faith-building.

The Word Is Very Near You: A Guide to Praying with Scripture, Martin L. Smith, Cambridge, MA: Cowley Publications, 1989. Just what it says.

Printed in the USA
CPSIA information can be obtained
at www.ICGtesting.com
JSHW051959150824
68134JS00057B/3481

9 781640 650312